Preface

Consciousness becoming conscious of itself is creation.

These were the words spoken by Sri Bhagavan when he was tweleve years old. The phenomenon of Sri Amma and Sri Bhagavan is unique in the annals of history in more ways than one. When a seeker asked Sri Bhagavan as to when and what experience in his life led him to the passion of enlightening mankind, Sri Bhagavan replied, "My first thoughts as a child had always been humanity and its condition. I have always known that I am different from the rest of mankind and I want to take mankind into a state beyond all division."

The unparalleled teachings and insights of Sri Bhagavan have liberated the listeners even as they heard them from Him when he was a little boy watching his friends in the play ground.

People over the years have often wondered

"Why it is that such a mammoth movement with such revolutionary and insightful teachings has had absolutely no literature to present to the world ?"

A single statement of Sri Bhagavan brings out the difficult of this task "Truth, when it is not yours still remains untruth."

Owing to the increasing request from seekers across the globe, the guides at the oneness university have now taken upon themselves the daunting task of presenting the teachings of Sri Amma and Sri Bhagavan to the world. That is why we are beginning in the reverse chronological order hoping to soon bring you the interactions Sri Amma and Sri Bhagavan have had with the seekers over the years.

∾

Introduction

“Evenings.. with Sri Bhagavan”, is a tiny compilation from the voluminous wisdom that pours forth from Him. These are answers to the questions posed by the seekers who participate in the various courses at the University. The sprawling lawn in front of Sri Bhagavan's residence is the regular venue for these Darshans.

These evenings with Sri Bhagavan are divine spectacles. One finds seekers moving into exalted states of consciousness even as they mediate in His Presence. Miracles in terms of healing of the mind and body are regular happenings. Participants are left spell bound or in ecstasy at the end of the darshans. Long after Sri Bhagavan's departure, seekers sway to a music that emerges from within their souls; hugging each other, tears coursing down their eyes; they are filled with the Presence of God. It is an experience that is a must for every mortal before he moves into the beyond.

It is a very humble on behalf of the guides at the University to enable the reader to get a feel of the liberating and practical teachings of Sri Amma and Sri Bhagavan and Their Grace that empowers the processes here.

Very little editing has been done in order to give an actual feel of the Darshans to the readers. The answers of Sri Bhagavan range from mind development and relationships to enlightenment and God; from the mysteries of creation to major shifts of paradigms in science. A very small range of subjects has been covered in this book deliberately because it is meant for the beginners. More subjects would be included in the forth-coming releases.

~

How do I make use of this book?

Most questions in this book are those that would have echoed the hearts of many. People on reviewing the book exclaimed, "These are what I dreamt I would ask God some day I chance to meet him.

Read the questions and answers carefully and mull over them. Every answer contains insights that would help in ending a lifetime's conflict and struggle. These teachings awaken and goad you on to the path of enlightenment and God realization. You would get in touch with the infinite compassion and Love of Sri Bhagavan. However, at this juncture, we would like to acquaint you with the central tenet of Sri Bhagavan, which is, "Man cannot make it on his own. It has to be given to him. Oneness is not a state to be achieved or practiced but a benediction to be received."

∾

How it all began...

The entrance proclaimed the vision of its founders. Jeevashram, a gurukula patashala, set amidst sylvan surroundings was the chosen place that cradled the divine phenomenon that later engulfed the whole world.

Along the alleys on either side were boards with profound insights on diverse aspects of life like relationships, parenting, right schooling, suffering, bondage and liberation. The campus echoed with the laughter of the children. The spiritual atmosphere of the patashala nurtured in the children a freedom of spirit and a tenderness of being.

Suddenly one day, strange happenings were spoken in whispers among the children, that a divine phenomenon had taken birth on the campus. The Golden Ball of Divine Grace had descended and a mystical phenomenon was unfolding itself, with the hitherto playful children turning into unbelievable prophets, miraculous healers, saints in divine communion, experiencing tremendous states of consciousness that had been a prerogative of a very few seers and sages of the past.

During one of these exciting days, a very active student of the school was walking back to the classroom after the lunch hour. Passing through the administrative blocks, he happened to glance through one of the rooms where Sri Bhagavan was seated. For a brief period their eyes met. The boy swooned and there after for three continuous days, the inmates witnessed the boy moving on and off into Nirvikalpa Samadhi. At last when the boy was becoming irretrievable, Sri Bhagavan Himself intervened and restored the boy back to his normal state. Such instances of children moving into extraordinary states were becoming common occurrences. Everyday some child or the other would pour forth revelations about future occurrences or expound with unmatched eloquence, the great insights of enlightened masters or emanate such silence, bliss and love from their being that it transported others too who were in touch with them.

The pinnacle of these glorious events was the awakening of the Antaryamin or the higher sacred self in the heart of a young student, Sri Krishnaji. When he laid his hands on the other children, the Golden Ball of Divine Grace descended in to them, putting them in touch with their higher sacred self. This mystical phenomenon later came to be known as the Deeksha. It has since become the way for millions of people across the globe, for whom a divine communion with God in their hearts has become a normal everyday affair.

It was during this phase that Sri Amma and Sri Bhagavan decided to reveal Their vision of creating a oneness age to the rest of the world. With the mission being carried unto the masses by the disciples, the movement started unfurling itself across the length and breadth of the nation. Scores of men and women, young and old alike partook of Sri Amma and Bhagavan's Divine Grace and got redeemed of their physical and mental afflictions, discovering a state of causeless love and limitless joy. Thus it began...

~

Our Beloved Mother Sri Amma

Nectar courses down the throats of millions of devotees even as they utter the word 'Amma'. Words are rendered meaningless in the compassionate and loving glance of Amma. Amma's smile and the look of benevolence are forever etched in the hearts of every one of its beholders. Amma's childlike innocence and immense wisdom instill in the hearts of the listeners, a tremendous reverence and an immediate affection towards Her. Very often, devotees are found either in irrepressible laughter or in silent tears, since Amma makes it known to them that she is indeed aware of their unspoken sorrows and hidden devotion.

Regular Darshans of Sri Amma are held at the Oneness Temple, Nemam, Tamil Nadu. These Darshans are occasions where Sri Amma showers Her Blessings upon the devotees gathered, answering their prayers and fulfilling their desires. The Darshans have led to a profound transformations in the lives of the participants several years of addiction and compulsive habits giving way, the blind getting sight, the lame starting to walk, families coming together; an end to years of loneliness, as they experience the Divine Presence in their heats.

~

Sepetember 15th 2004

Seeker: What is the vision or the purpose of the Oneness University?

Sri Bhagavan: This university is a university for universities. It is to make you into a true human being. Other universities give you technical knowledge. They give you specialisation, but they never make you into a human being; into what you are supposed to be. Every human being has to be enlightened. Every human being has to be God realised. This university exists to help you become enlightened, to help you become God realised. But down the line if you have got specific problems, we are prepared to deal with that also. The full flowering of the human being is nothing but the flowering of the heart. Society must be so structured that the heart of the child does not wither away. Sadly today, the way parents conceive children, bring them up in the womb, the way they deliver them in the hospitals and the way they bring up the children in the schools, in the colleges, in the society, everything destroys the child. That is why there are no human beings.

There was once a great saint, in Chennai city, about a century ago. He used to sit in front of his house and when people went by, he would say, "here goes a dog, here goes a fox, here goes a pig, here goes a donkey". Only on one occasion, throughout his life he said, "here goes a man" and that was for Ramalinga Swamy, a great saint who disappeared into light. Only he was qualified to be called 'man' by him. All the others were animals,to him.

Do you see all the barbarity in the world? How barbarous we are, how primitive we are? We have divided ourselves on the basis of race, on the basis of nations, on the basis of cults, on the basis of wealth; in fact all kinds of division. We keep fighting in the name of God, in the name of religion, in the name of love. How many wars we have fought - tribal wars, national wars, world wars. Only a species that is completely mad could behave the way we are behaving. Otherwise how could you kill a fellow human being brutally and take away his things and think of the silent torture that goes on in homes, man nagging his wife, woman nagging her husband. Everybody exploiting the other, wanting to dominate the other. Wife wants to dominate the husband, husband wants to dominate the wife; children want to dominate the parents and they in turn want to dominate the children. Employee over employer, employer over employee. Everywhere you turn, the self is at play. This is hell. There is no other hell.

So, the question is one of simple transformation. Make the heart flower and we have heaven here. There will be actual Heaven on Earth.

∾

∾

Seeker: Bhagavan, how to control the mind? How to make use of the immense power of the mind?

Sri Bhagavan: How to control the mind? I wonder if this is ever possible! Since the more you try to control the mind, the more it would go out of control and in the ensuing battle, you are sure to be the loser. If somebody ever fights the mind, it always wins, because as he fights with the mind, it takes away his strength and becomes stronger. The only way you could become free of the mind is to closely watch it. If you keep watching it in a very friendly way without judging, condemning or commenting, it soon becomes very weak and slowly becomes quieter.

∾

∾

Seeker: Bhagavan, during the process we realized that all of us are filled with nothing but self centeredness. Did you create us this way or did something go wrong with us, Bhagavan?

Sri Bhagavan: Nobody created you like this, least of all, Me. It is a part of the times that keep changing. The mind arises and the mind ceases. In Satyayuga, your mind sort of ceases, it comes back in the other yugas and becomes very strong in Kaliyuga. This is neither your fault nor mine. Neither you wanted it, nor did I want it. I am as helpless as you are.

∾

~

Seeker: Bhagavan, does an enlightened person suffer? What would be his response to another's suffering?

Sri Bhagavan: When we say you are free of suffering, what it means is that you are free of personal suffering. You do suffer. The Buddha suffered, Christ suffered, everybody suffers. Only thing is once enlightened, it is no more 'your' suffering. It is the suffering of mankind that touches you and you just cannot keep quiet. You would respond to it. Right now, if somebody else is suffering, you hardly sense it and even when you do sense, you are very protective about yourself. When you are enlightened, you do not think and act, you just act. What the response would be, nobody could tell. It could vary from one day to another. Mankind's suffering becomes your suffering. It is no more personal suffering.

~

∾

Seeker: Bhagavan, would the unconscious mind trouble us even after the heart flowers?

Sri Bhagavan: As you grow spiritually, the unconscious loses its grip over you in phases, in degrees. The flowering of the heart is a very important milestone on the spiritual path. This flowering of the heart and the love which accompanies it, is not the kind of love you are normally used to. Once the heart has flowered, you know exactly how to act. Even if you do have that love, you still are not enlightened. However, for those whose heart has flowered, enlightenment is round the corner. They could make it any time.

∾

~

Seeker: Bhagavan, why does not the world get transformed easily? Is the penance done by our ancestors going to help us in anyway on our spiritual path?

Sri Bhagavan: As I have told you earlier, it is not your fault that you are not transformed. We are all product of the times. Fortunately, the times have changed; we have entered wonderful times and people by and large are easily going to make it. It is not that they must come here; it is not that they must undergo a process. Initially a few of you would have to come for this process then you will be able to go back and give it to people. Your power would be growing very fast week by week, month by month, year by year. Then probably a touch would do, a look would do. So, you would transform people. Then there would come a point where nobody needs to touch another and people would automatically make it. The wall called the mind would crumble on its own. It is not going to take long. The only thing is, by becoming enlightened, by helping others become enlightened, we are helping this process. Since we are part of this process, we are part of nature, we should co-operate, nature expects us to co-operate. We are giving it a helping hand. Even otherwise manlind's discretion is just an event which will come to pass. Mankind would have moved into other ages.

When we suffered in the earlier ages, again nobody was responsible, we had to. It is not that our great great grandfathers suffered that we are fortunate. No! We were those great great grandfathers. We have come back, will again come back. We are only rotating again and again. We have been recycled. So, we have worked hard for many many years, I think now it is time to reap the harvest. That's why, I maintain it does not matter who you are or, what you are. Whether you are a sinner or a saint does not matter because everybody is going to make it.

~

∾

Seeker: Bhagavan, You have shown me how Amma and Bhagavan have been by my side, guiding me through out my life. Have You been working with us for many life times? If so, how many?

Sri Bhagavan: Yes, countless number of times. Actually even though I began My work probably about fourteen years ago, I have appeared to people and worked with them in this form even before I was born. There are people living, who have met Me even before I was born. This has been going on for countless ages.

∾

∾

Seeker: Bhagavan, I have discovered I am relating to You because of my self centeredness. I feel bad about it .

Sri Bhagavan: It is perfectly fine. I do not mind your self centeredness. However, there would come a time when even without this self centeredness, you would still perfectly relate to Me. Now that it is there, relate. I do not mind your self-centeredness at all. Remember one thing, I cannot judge you. You cannot be judged because you are not responsible, the self is there and it has to protect itself. It has its needs, necessities, therefore it is seeking. It is perfectly fine. That is why I am ready to answer your desires. The only thing is, it should not hurt or harm somebody else. That is all.

∾

Seeker: Bhagavan, how does the relationship with the Divine change as we move into higher states? As we go on becoming one with the Divine, would we cease to exist?

Sri Bhagavan: You see, as you go on progressing, you would find that one minute you are God yourself and the next minute you are not. What happens is after sometime you would realize that actually you and God are the same. But, sometimes you would have the feeling of Oneness, sometimes you would have a feeling of separation. It is then you could be of very great help to people. This is possible to be achieved in this life-time itself and there are people who have achieved this. I am not talking of anything which at least a few people have not achieved. That is why we are talking about oneness. You would actually discover that you are one with the Divine, that you are actually God. This continues on a regular basis. The only thing is as you go along, the time you experience Oneness with God would be more.

You would actually become Amma Bhagavan or Light or God or whatever you want to call it;What form the Divine would take for you depends upon you. When you still go deeper, your physical form could also be affected. There is no end to these things. They happen very naturally, very automatically. I suggest you read about Ramalinga Swami. It is a very beautiful example of how somebody became one with God. He lived in very recent times and his life is very well recorded. He lived in the city of Chennai. It would give you a good idea as to what possibilities exist in the domain of the Presence because I have not known anything equivalent to that in any other literature of the world and so very modern also. That state would become yours. In fact he tried to give to others, but for some reason he could not. When he had to face opposition in his work he said "Now I'm going back. However, I will come back with my father whom you cannot take for a ride."

∾

~

Seeker: Bhagavan, how is the country's prosperity linked with the enlightenment of people?

Sri Bhagavan: There are a lot of mental blocks, especially for the Indians, which are making this country such a poor country. As we become enlightened, these mental blocks would disappear and with the disappearance of the mental blocks, the very thinking would change and the country would naturally become prosperous. What is the problem with India? The thinking is defective. The mind set has to be changed. Somehow we have begun to worship poverty, we seem to relish failure. We seem to glorify all these negative things. I do not want to go into where exactly it started in history. There was a point of time when all this began in India. Before that you must know India was a very very prosperous and a very very healthy country. If you read about Marco polo's travels in India, he says, if you met somebody on the road and gave him a huge amount of gold, even if you came back after ten years, the man would return it to you. Nobody would cheat you. That was the wealth of the country. So how did it become so poor? Something went wrong with the thinking. I have spoken about this earlier. Once you become enlightened, this thinking would change. Once the thinking changes, you automatically become prosperous. Poverty begins in the mind.

∾

∾

Seeker: Bhagavan, we all love You so much.

Sri Bhagavan: Thank you. You must know that I love you much more than you love Me. You have no idea how much I love you. Sometimes when I see you suffering, I can't take it. When I am with My disciples, I do in fact weep. My love for you is the motivation to do this work. You just don't know how much I and Amma love you.

∾

Sepetember 23rd 2004

∾

Seeker: Bhagavan, what is the difference between thought and mind? Is the mind more powerful than the thoughts and does the mind control thoughts? Please explain to us.

Sri Bhagavan: Well! If you take a building, it is made of bricks. Without bricks, you do not have the building. Similar are the mind and thoughts. How you could have a mind without thoughts. So, you can't really separate the two. The mind is nothing but the flow of thoughts, which is a flow of memory. If we were to remove your memory, there is no mind at all. You cannot conceive of a mind, without thoughts.

∾

~

Seeker: What is love? Is it crush or affection or emotion?

Sri Bhagavan: I cannot tell you what 'love' is. I can tell you what love is not. Crush is not love, emotion is not love, attachment is not love, possession is not love. You go on saying, I will be saying no, no, no. The love we are talking about cannot be described. It has to be experienced. There is no use talking about it. Because all that you know is conditional. This love I am talking about is totally unconditional; there is no reason for that. There is no cause for that. It is just there. We would like you to get there. You would then be a fulfilled human being. You would have realised your full potential as a human being. Otherwise you are not a human being at all because the moment you discover this love, you also discover connectedness. You feel connected with your parents, with your brothers, friends and everybody else in the world. Right now you do not have this connectedness. That is why I say, 'everybody is an orphan'. You do not feel connected even to your parents, to your spouses. Your lives are miserable, lonely, meaningless because you lead unconnected lives. When this love is there, you feel connected. First you feel connected with your near and dear ones, with your friends, then with the world at large, plants and animals and finally with God. You become one with God. That is the oneness we are talking about.

So, if you do not have this connectedness, life is just not worth living. Love has to be discovered. It has to happen. You just cannot do anything about it. I can give it. I am not saying that I am the only one who could give it. When you give Deekshas you would also be able to give it.

∾

~

Seeker: Bhagavan, What happens in the Phala-Deeksha?

Sri Bhagavan: In the Phala-Deeksha you come face to face with God. God itself is many things. God is emptiness, God is light, God is universal consciousness, God is collective human consciousness, God is the Antaryamin, God is both male and female. Then God is the Avatar. So, God is at several levels. In the Phala-Deeksha, you are coming face to face with God as collective human consciousness. He can take any form. He can either come as a presence, as a light, as Amma Bhagavan, as Rama, Krishna, Christ, or whatever God you worship. What form God takes depends on you. We are basically dealing with collective human consciousness which manifests as the Antaryamin.

In the Phala-Deeksha you can ask God for your heart to be awakened, for your relationships to be set right, to discover love, an altered state of consciousness, enlightenment and God realisation. Dependent on any number of factors, He would say 'Yes' or 'No' to your prayers. In other words, in the Phala-Deeksha you are in touch with God.

∾

~

Seeker: What are Fundamental Childhood Decisions(FCD's)? How do they control our life?

Sri Bhagavan: These are the basic decisions which happen in the womb, in the first few hours after delivery and the first few years after that. They vary from child to child. And these decisions in fact form the blue print which controls the rest of life. The whole secret lies there. That is why to change the course of life, we would have to tamper with the fundamental childhood decisions which is not very difficult at all. It can be done quite easily.

~

~

Seeker: Bhagavan, when everything is destined by the divine, what should be my role?

Sri Bhagavan: Well! Your role is to execute the divine plan. That is all. Each of you is intended for a specific purpose and it is possible to discover your destiny. The best thing is to work to fulfill that destiny. And the best thing is to do that. It does not matter what you are asked to do. But if you do what you have been asked to do, there is enormous ecstasy.

~

~

Seeker: Bhagavan, what is the dream plane that we enter at night. Is it real or illusiory?

Sri Bhagavan: Sometimes an average human being while dreaming in the night, could also move into the astral world. The astral world is quite real and is in fact ahead of time as compared to planetary time. Sometimes when people die, they are born on the astral plane and then when they die in the astral plane, they come back to the earth plane. When you die in the astral plane you move into the higher planes and when you die in the higher plane you are reborn in the astral plane. That is how you keep progressing, till you finally go into the highest plane and there you stay for all time. That is how people generally progress. But almost everybody spends sometime in the night in the astral plane. The astral plane of course also contains terrible places. It is not that it is all so wonderful. There are places which are not so nice. If you visit them, you would feel very tired in the morning, because you would have certainly been participating in some boxing match there. Lots of fighting goes on in many places. In fact if we were to show you what you did in those worlds, you will know how terrible you are. You inhibit all your pent up violence. You could have been knocked down by someone there. The next morning you would find yourself very exhausted and tired after a full night's sleep. There are ofcourse many beautiful places also. Some times, you could even remember them after waking.

∾

~

Seeker: Bhagavan, lot of young children die of diseases like cancer, brain tumours etc. What is the reason for this? Has this to do with Karma or is it that the child only had to live a few years on the planet for some learning? Could you tell me something about this and how we could help it?

Sri Bhagavan: This is happening basically because man is so very violent and because of what you are doing to the earth. For example, you take a big eucalyptus plantation, the trees are growing, and you take the bulldozer and you cut the whole thing down. Then you have these poultry farms, dairy farms, where you torture animals. You actually prevent them from leading their full life. You terminate them. You take them to the abattoir, you kill them. What about the goat and the sheep! Each species has a role to play in this web of life and human beings are intended to protect the environment. But man is doing exactly the opposite. His role is to protect the earth, the animals, the plants, all the species, but he is hardly doing that. Instead, he has started consuming them all. He thinks they are all meant for him. The amount of cruelty that is being practiced cannot be described at all. That is what is coming back as cancer, all these infant deaths and the terrible things which you are now seeing. You are going to see probably more of them unless of course mankind changes. Nature is hitting back and if nature really starts becoming furious, you had it! You could all be wiped off like ants... We only hope that man becomes enlightened very soon and transforms himself.

∾

~

Seeker: What is the best course to follow when one encounters suffering. Bhagavan, please also give us more clarity on what is 'running away from suffering'.

Sri Bhagavan: Well! There is no need to give clarity on running away from suffering, because you are doing it all the time. Whenever you say I am suffering, it means you are running away from suffering. Because if you could turn around and confront suffering, soak in it, embrace it, fall in love with it, be with it, accept it; Then you will, see for yourself, what happens!

~

~

Seeker: Everyone seems to be alright with the feeling of love, affection, oneness and seva in this sacred surrounding. But when one goes to the material and busy world,would we not get lost in conflict and turmoil once again? Please Bhagavan, tell us the right way, which would not only help us remain as noble human beings, but would also set us as examples in society and help in creating a better society and a peaceful world?

Sri Bhagavan: I cannot speak to you about any right way or right path. We are speaking about a permanent transformation, which would hold good wherever you are. It does not matter whether you are in this atmosphere or you are in the world outside. The key thing here is for you to get into a state where seeing is occurring all the time. That is what we are trying to do in the courses here. When seeing happens, all suffering ceases because to see is to be free.

There is no effort involved, there is no time involved. The example that we often give is, supposing there were to be a snake in front of you, you would be very scared and would shiver in fear. The moment you see it is not a snake but a rope, instantly the fear is gone. No time is involved, no effort is involved. You see and are free. The same thing applies to what is going on within the mind. If you could really see what is going on, what ever that might be, whether it be a lustful thought or a murderous thought, or any kind of thought; there is only joy and freedom. 'What is there' is not important. The only thing is - to 'see' what ever is going on?

Since it is only seeing, we do not call it 'the path' or 'the right path'. We don't use such words. That is why we often say there is no path here.

∾

~

Seeker: How should I confront my self centeredness, Bhagavan?

Sri Bhagavan: There is no 'how'. You just become aware of your self centeredness. It is there, that is all. You are not going to condemn it. The basic thing is, you are all the time either justifying, finding reasons to explain why this is so or are condemning it. It is just a fact. And if you would look at it like that, something strange happens. There is nothing you need to do. So, confronting your self centeredness, though the word is misleading means that you just become aware that this is what you really are and you never thought you are that. It is so and it is there, that is all. The mere seeing is sufficient.

~

~

Seeker: Bhagavan, what is the purpose of creation?

Sri Bhagavan: Well, we could answer it from different contexts. When you do become enlightened, you realise that there is no purpose to this creation. It is just there. It is just there because there is too much of joy in creation and that joy is expressing itself in all these forms. There is no purpose. That is why I often give an example of people going to a cricket match. They see somebody hitting a big six and you find people jumping up and screaming. There is no purpose to that. You can't ask what is the use of jumping and screaming. They jumped up and screamed because there was too much of joy. Whole of creation is an outpouring of joy. Once you become enlightened, you will see that there is nothing but joy. There is only love.

~

∾

Seeker: Why this passion in you Bhagavan to give enlightenment to man?

Sri Bhagavan: Look at your life. You are born, you go to school, there is a lot of competition there, you have to study for your exams, get the marks. Your parents are worried, you cause worry to them, you are under stress. All that is over. You go to college, again it is the same strife, then you fall in love with somebody, you are not able to marry her or marry him, that thing goes on, then again frustration. Finally you get a job, there you may be happy or may not be happy. Again competition, no promotion, stress and strain. In the end you get married. You are happy for three months, then the problem starts. Then, you beget children, take them to school again, then go to some movies, watch television, read newspapers, magazines, eat some food, go for picnics. Is there anything to your life at all? You take everyday the same coffee, the same breakfast and lunch and dinner; may be a slight variation. What is there to your life? So, as far as I am concerned you are merely existing, you are not living. You exist because you are afraid to die. All of you would like to become the Prime Minister of India, is it possible? No. All of you would like to become the CEO of a company, is it possible? No. No, no, no, no. You have to make compromises and adjust, this and that. What is there to your life? Other than the terrible struggles!

All right, let us say you make money, a lot of money; I have met a lot of wealthy people who tell me clearly, Bhagavan we are in deep depression. Money has not given them happiness, it is too sickening and boring after a point of time. They are searching here and there. So, successful people too are not happy. Whether you achieve success or not, you are not happy. Either way you are not happy. As long as you are there, whether you are a failure or a success in life the end result is the same. You are not going to be happy. Because if you are

there, your being there is unhappiness. Not that you are unhappy. No. You = unhappiness. That is your condition. So, how long can this go on? This has been going on from two million years.
Now, what is enlightenment? It is wiping out the 'you'. We give Deeksha and wipe you out. If you are gone, you will still be very functional. The memory is there, you can do everything you are doing, only much better. Since you are not there, what is there is joy, happiness, and love. It does not matter whether you are the chairman or a clerk of a company. There was a big Guru in North India who was a peon in the high court. Daily during evenings like this he had satsang. In the satsang, the judge would be sitting down and he would be giving his discourse. Next day in the morning, the judge would be on the chair and he would be holding the records. The judge would be shivering because his Guru was standing. So the Guru said, 'look! here I am a peon, I will stand, you do your duty'. But the peon was much happier than the judge who was sitting there. While I could help some people to

become CEOs and rich, what about the millions who cannot be helped? Even if I am going to make you into a CEO, you are still going to be unhappy. The peon also is going to be unhappy. But I want people to be happy. What should we do? We should erase you. Once 'you' are gone, it does not matter who you are, what you are, what is there is only joy and happiness.

If there is joy and happiness in you, would you cause trouble to others? Never. Only an unhappy person would cause trouble to somebody else. If all over the world people are happy, would there be any problem in the external world? If, this inner transformation which we call oneness happens, there will also be a corresponding change in the external world. Everybody would be happy, there would be no crime, there would be no conflict. This inner change is what we are calling, 'Oneness age'. The external change the 'Golden Age'.

∾

~

Seeker: How do we bring about an understanding relationship?

Sri Bhagavan: No amount of psychology or philosophy would set right relationships. In the first place, trying to understand a relationship would never help. Trying to understand is like peeling an onion; you could go on peeling, at the end, there would be nothing left of it. You must learn the art of experiencing the other. If you learn to experience your husband or your wife, there is no greater joy than that, on this planet. But the problem is you do not know how to experience human beings; you do not feel connected. I have often given an example of a couple, of a doctor who married vegetable vendor as his wife. A woman, who was exceptionally ugly, who used only foul language and was very filthy. It is twenty five years since they were married. They are the best couple I have seen because the doctor experiences her every moment. He preferred her among all the well bred fashionable women becuase, he knew that if she were his wife, he could experience her. That is why he married her and vice versa. So, people do not know how to experience each other. If you know how to experience your wife. Even if she were to nag you or to scream or yell at you, it would be a most beautiful experience. Similarly, when your husband also bothers you, if you can see and experience him, it becomes joy. That is the only way you can set right your relationship because then it becomes a source of joy. In the courses here, we are also trying to teach you how to experience the other, to feel connected. It looks a bit difficult, but not really. If it is too difficult, we would'nt talk about it. Many people are already doing this.

∾

~

Seeker: How is Your dharma different from the other dharmas?

Sri Bhagavan: We are helping people discover the truths embodied by their faiths. As far as we are concerned, we are not trying to produce any synchristic faith, by putting them all together. We are trying to keep each faith as pure as possible, as it originally was; because all faiths are experience based. That is how faiths start. But soon the existing powers take over and make use of them for other purposes. That is how they go corrupt, they become organised and finally they become a nuisance to mankind. We want to go back to their pristine purity. That is why at the oneness meditation hall which is more of a powerhouse, you could worship any God in any form you like. There will be a throne there, a very special kind of a throne where many could actually see the God they worship. The throne would be empty but you could see the God you worship. I don't think this dharma or movement has any independent existence.

~

Seeker: Bhagavan, what is oneness within oneself?

Sri Bhagavan: Oneness within oneself is the cessation of the inner dialogue. Right now if you watch yourself, you would find a crowd inside. You would find yourself being the father of so and so, the son of so and so, the husband of so and so, the brother of so and so, the friend of so and so. And all these beings are talking all the time. That is why I often refer to you as a mobile market place. When you achieve true oneness, this inner dialogue between these personalities stops. Then there is an inner silence which is not the opposite of noise, it is something else. That is inner oneness.

~

Seeker: Could you please tell us something about seeing?

Sri Bhagavan: Yes, the first thing is seeing. Seeing is the key thing in the dharma. When it comes to inner problems or inner growth or spiritual progress, you have to learn the art of seeing. Supposing jealousy is there, you must learn to see jealousy. We are not concerned about jealousy as such. What is there is not important for us, but you must 'see' what is there. 'To see is to be free'. It is not to be understood as freedom from jealousy; the mere act of seeing jealousy is freedom. This freedom is meditation. It is joy. It is peace. It is love.

~

~

Seeker: Bhagavan, how exactly do we experience suffering?

Sri Bhagavan: When we use the word 'suffering' what we mean is 'you are running away from suffering. That is what you call suffering' and you are not aware of it. Supposing somebody is dead in your house, your near or dear one. You do not want to face that fact, and hence keep running away from it. That is what you call suffering. Not the actual thing which happened. On the other hand if you were to turn around and embrace the event that happened, initially it could be tremendously painful, you could even develop chest pain. Some times the body itself could become very violent and go into convulsions as you embrace suffering. Without internally moving away from suffering or trying to understand it, not trying to explain it away jump into it. This is what we call jumping into the tiger's mouth. At the moment you are hanging on to the ceiling and the tiger is growling and you are afraid that you might fall anytime into the tiger's mouth. That is what you call suffering. What we are telling is please jump down from the ceiling straight into the tiger's mouth and be eaten. Strangely if you are eaten, you are gone, who is there to suffer? That is why we say, you do not have to understand suffering. You do not have to bring in psychology and philosophy, they would never help you in disolving your suffering. They would only help you escape. If not experienced the tiger is going to pounce on you some other day. The best thing is to embrace it and the strangest part is you will find sooner or later you will develop this art and every time suffering comes, you would embrace it and it would become joy. One who has completely mastered the art of converting suffering into joy is almost enlightened. Not enlightened but almost enlightened!

∾

~

Seeker: Bhagavan, why are You suffering and struggling so much for our sake, why do You love us so much?

Sri Bhagavan: To me there is no sense of separateness at all. When I see you, you are not different from me. You could be a stranger who has just arrived from some part of the world, but to me you are no stranger. I feel completely connected with you. It is like my talking to myself. Whoever you are, does not matter.

So, questions like why am I trying to help you do not arise because I am not helping anybody. I am just helping myself. I cannot see you as something other than me. For functional purposes I might use the word I, you, this, that. It is a real experience, and not something you could conceptualise. I do not have the feeling that I am working for somebody. I can't work for anybody, there is no body out there for me. What I am trying to give you is my own state. In that state, there is no sense of separateness, but only connectedness. The whole problem with mankind is, people do not feel connected. They neither feel connected to their husbands or wives nor to their children or parents, nor to nature. There is no connectedness at all. There is complete isolation and separateness; that is the misery which mankind is undergoing.

To escape this misery, he is trying to create all kinds of things like social work, various movements, all kinds of things. I am not condemning them, they are okay. But it is of little use. Unless and until you handle this misery of man, nothing is going to really work and if you could handle this, there is no need for all that. It does not mean that I am telling you people "Oh! Stop doing all this work", no! Since you are not enlightened, it is necessary. Continue with them, get some good results out of them. That is why though you had the French revolution, the American revolution, the Russian revolution, you have not gone anywhere at all.

Human beings continues to be the same, the objects of desire could have changed but desire continues. The reasons for fear could have changed, he could have feared the tiger in olden times, now he fears the share market. So, fear continues. Basically there is no transformation in man. There is tremendous misery and all this is out of a sense of separateness. Your lives are meaningless and purposeless. There is only misery but you are all expert managers of suffering. You all have got an MBA in the management of suffering and you somehow beautifully manage it. You have newspapers, television, your discos, you go to restaurants and eat so much that most of you are sick. You have developed all the wrong living habits. You are destroying yourself because you are not able to handle this misery in you.

So, this is the condition. You have to loose the sense of separation and to feel connected. First you start with your own family, then the world. Then you extend it to the animals, plants and then finally to God. That is why we use the word oneness. Oneness starts basically within yourself, you are one with yourself. Right now you are a stranger unto yourself. You don't love yourself, forget loving others, it is pointless. That is why start with oneness there, then it moves on and finally ends with oneness with God. When we speak of oneness with God, we mean actually becoming one with God. It is no concept, not a way of speaking but an actuality. People are already there and that is what you should be doing.

∾

October 2nd 2004

~

Seeker: In several movements, people speak about surrendering oneself to God. What does this surrender mean according to you, Bhagavan?

Sri Bhagavan: It is not some kind of a slavish surrender. It is never used in that sense. God would not like you to surrender like a slave. He is after all your friend. So, when we use the word surrender it means setting aside the mind, knowing its limitations.

~

∾

Seeker: Karma requires cause and effect. Cause and effect require time. Time is an illusion, so how could there be Karma?

Sri Bhagavan: That is why Karma also is an illusion. If you have this insight, Karma cannot touch you. Karma is there only as long as you have the illusion that it is there. But if you can really see that it is not there, it no more touches you. However, it must be an experience for you.

∾

∾

Seeker: Why is it that negative energies and negative thoughts enter the mind more easily than positive energy and positive thoughts? Why is the mind designed like this? Why cannot you change this design of the mind?

Sri Bhagavan: Yes! That has to do with the Yuga in which we are living. That is the nature of Kaliyuga. However, you can be happy that Kaliyuga has ended. The Golden Age has arrived. For all the negative things that you hear in the world, there are also some wonderful things happening.

∾

∾

Seeker: Bhagavan, you have control on everything, then why do you say Karma is ours. You could have controlled us before things went wrong. Why did you come so late?

Sri Bhagavan: You must understand the nature of God and His powers and limitations. That is why I think the best way to answer this question is; to give you the experience of becoming God for a short while in this process. That is the way you will know how to handle these questions. You must also know my difficulties. I was explaining the other day, about a girl who was praying for one thing and her mother who had an opposite prayer. What do I do in a situation like that? It is very complex. Only if you are in my situation you would know what it is like. These questions are cropping up more frequently these days; I think the best thing would be to give you an experience.

∾

~

Seeker: How different should our attitude be to receive grace for the inner world and the outer world?

Sri Bhagavan: There is absolutely no contradiction. For spiritual growth and getting in touch with yourself you must start with where you are. On the other hand when you want to fulfill worldly desires, you must change the situation. What is applied to the inner world should not be applied to the external world. In the inner world you do nothing. In the external world you must do everything. Where desires are concerned with the external world, you must tell me - 'I want this,' ' I want that.' Very often people are unclear about what they want. Unless you are clear I cannot act. Even as you keep thinking you contradict yourself. You are vague. That is why I am not able to act. Understand there is no contradiction. In the inner world, you stay where you are. If there is jealousy, you stay with it. That is all. That is the only truth. You cannot say I will be free of jealousy. It is not possible. There is only jealousy. While in the external world if you want to buy a house, or earn some money, you want to get this, or that. The best thing would be ask for it.

~

~

Seeker: Could you please explain to me how grace is linked to inner integrity?

Sri Bhagavan: The moment there is inner integrity; your link with the Lord is firmly established. It is very easy for grace to flow. When there is no inner integrity, the contact is not clear. It becomes very difficult to give you grace because as far as Bhagavan is concerned He is very eager to give grace to anybody and everybody. However, the problem is with regards to the connection. The connection is more like a telecom line. It would be proper only, if there were inner integrity. That is how it helps you. In fact, you could yourself do miracles if you were integral.

~

∾

Seeker: You said that you are one with all of us. If so, how could you experience some people who are suffering and some people who are happy all at the same time? Please explain your nature to us Bhagavan.

Sri Bhagavan: There is no way you could understand My nature. As far as you are concerned, you have limitations of space and time. You feel you are limited to the body and that the other is separate. These things do not exist for me. I do not feel you are separate at all. To know what it exactly is you must get the experience, which I would be giving you. Then you would know for yourself. You would experience reality in a totally different way. It is possible to actually feel an animal, you could feel what the ant is thinking, and many more things. However, since you are not used to it you think that it is impossible. You assume you are separate. No body is separate from the other. You are all just one being. So, the ultimate objective is to give you that state of consciousness, which some people have achieved probably for a few days or for a few hours in a day. But slowly people are emerging who are fully in this state all the time. Very soon, I feel a large number of people would be able to experience it almost all the time. It is possible.

∾

Seeker: When I see the Srimurthi, something attracts me. What is the secret behind this Bhagavan?

Sri Bhagavan: I am in the Srimurthi. You must know that I am alive in the Srimurthi. It is not a mere picture. Sometimes blood could come out of the Srimurthi in case you have been saved somewhere. It is a living picture. It has life. There are Srimurthis which weep, there are Srimurthis which laugh. Two Bhagavans could actually talk also. They have distinct personalities having lived with you. His Bhagavan would acquire a particular personality; Your Bhagavan would acquire a different personality, and they could be talking also. Sometimes you could tune into what they are talking. It is a living thing. That is why you feel the Presence so much. Of course some Srimurthis could be deserted also. They would be lifeless, if not worshiped or regarded.

∾

∾

Seeker: How does Nara become Narayana?

Sri Bhagavan: Nara becomes Narayana when he achieves complete oneness. When the wall called the mind is gone then Nara becomes Narayana. There are saints and sages who have become one with Narayana and they have written about their experience.

∾

~

Seeker: How do we ordinary mortals, believe that you are God, Bhagavan?

Sri Bhagavan: I am not asking you to believe that I am God. I am asking you to discover that there is a God. And then let us see what happens. I am not asking you to start with the premise that I am God. But I maintain there is a God and you should discover who 'He' or 'She' or 'It' is.

~

Seeker: Bhagavan, you are changing the fate written by Brahma. Why do you not tell Brahma to write a good fate in the beginning itself, Bhagavan?

Sri Bhagavan: Nobody is writing. You are writing your destiny yourself.

~

Seeker: Whatever we do, is full of selfishness. Then how could we earn Sat-karma?

Sri Bhagavan: Out of pure selfishness you could help people and earn Sat karma. You could be very clear you want to earn Sat-karma and hence are helping others. That is how Karma works. You do not have to be unselfish at all. Supposing your eyesight is very bad, you could go to an eye hospital and pay off the bills of the needy or do some seva there, with the full intent that you want your eyesight to improve. You would find an improvement. When the self is there, there is nothing wrong in acting in a selfish way. Please get the whole thing straight. We are not asking you to be free of the self. We are only asking you to be conscious of the self. Helping you to be free of the self is my business. You cannot do it to yourself.

~

~

Seeker: Why inequality in creation Bhagavan? Some intelligent, some foolish, some capable, some incapable, why this difference?

Sri Bhagavan: What is wrong with it? That makes it very interesting. Inequality is not the problem... That you have a self is the problem. When there is no self all humanity would be one big family. The intelligent would help the weak, the rich would help the poor, it would be one family. So, inequality is not the problem at all. Nevertheless if somebody is unequal, he would be superior in some other way. It is compensated. But the problem is, the self. The solution is to do away with the self.

~

∾

Seeker: What are you Bhagavan? Teacher, Guru or God!

Sri Bhagavan: I am what you think I am.

∾

What is the Oneness University?

Two of the most cherished dreams of human life are success and love. An observation into our lives shows that while some of us are very successful certain others are not as successful as they would like to be. Many times we have tried to find out the reason for this disparity. Years of study by scientists and spiritual scholars alike has shown that a person's early childhood influences his later life in a major way. An insight into the factors that influence one's present day condition would unravel the secrets, education, relationships or spiritual sadhana.

In the words of the Divine Avatar Sri Bhagavan, "A human being's life is governed by his conditionings, fundamental childhood decisions, the experiences that happened in the womb and their previous incarnations.

For any qualitative change to occur in his life,

either one or all of these factors have to be worked upon. An unlearning of previous decisions and binding concepts is necessary to push one forward on the path of success and thereafter on to the path of God realisation and Oneness. The Oneness University is a centre for learning inspired by the Divine Avatars Sri Amma and Sri Bhagavan. The uniqueness of this university is that each one of the teachings imparted in the courses can also be experienced personally and verified by the participant. It's ultimate vision is to set man totally and unconditionally free and set him on the path of discovering oneness with God. He discovers that he is not only a part of God but that he is God.

∾

Why Oneness?

You are divided within yourself. You are torn within trying to choose between the good and the bad, the right and the wrong, the perfect and the imperfect. Society has put into you various ideals and hence life has become a constant struggle to live up to these ideals.

You neither feel one nor connected one with your loved ones, with nature or God. You exist in a state of alienation from all life. This division is the source of all strife that exists between individuals, families and cultures, religions and nations. In the words of Sri Bhagavan, "The only solution to all human problems and suffering is a state of oneness; oneness within oneself, with the world around and with God."

∾

About the University

The needs and aspirations of every individual are different. Some seek solutions to their problems and a fulfilment of their desires. Some others seek love and harmony in relationships while others seek enlightenment and God realisation.

The university helps you by helping you understand the root of your problem and helps you dissolve it by bestowing upon you the requisite knowledge and experience. All these are happenings in the basic and the advanced courses at the university, through the Deekshas of Amma and Bhagavan. (The Deeksha is a phenomenon where the Avatars through the power of their consciousness bestow upon the seeker, an altered state of consciousness.)

∾

The Oneness Process

The various courses offered at the university:

Oneness Process for Foreign Individuals

The oneness process is a divine benediction of Sri Amma and Bhagavan to all spiritual seekers aiming to ascend to a higher state of consciousness. This process involves a combination of teachings, sadhanas (meditation practices), ancient rituals and meditating in the presence of cosmic beings who are in a higher state of consciousness. These meditations and rituals act as a bridge between the seeker and the divine culminating in the awakening and the discovery of the divine. According to Sri Amma and Bhagavan divine grace is indispensable for this process.

This process opens the doors to the divine presence, which makes healing, liberation and other mystical phenomena possible. This awakening to the presence is characterized by profound insights and altered states of consciousness, paving the way for the flowering of the heart, a profound transformation in perceptions about life and the nature of the communication with the divine.

According to Sri Amma and Bhagavan, this awakening to the divine is not one fixed experience, but exists at various levels and can manifest differently to different people. The grace of the Divine has made it possible for innumerable seekers in India and abroad, from all walks of life, to experience different altered states of consciousness. Participants of the Oneness process are further initiated in service of mankind, by transferring the ability to give deekshas and effect a similar inner transformation in other seekers back home. World over, the participants of the Oneness process conduct deeksha sessions helping many more seekers to attain to their cherished goal of oneness.

The Oneness process is conducted for different groups belonging to different nationalities all year round. Adjacent to the Oneness Temple in Batthalavallam is the Golden City Phase -2 campus, which houses the Oneness Process for all international seekers. This campus is impregnated with certain very high energies conductive for ascension in consciousness and transformation. Fully air conditioned accommodation, spacious enough to accommodate 10-14 participants per room are available. Meditation halls generate a very serene and pleasant atmosphere for contemplation and meditation. The seekers would be provided with choicest sattvic vegetarian food throughout the process. Spiritual Guides of the Oneness University, who have been specially trained and prepared by Sri Amma and Bhagavan over the years, attend to the spiritual and functional needs of the participants.

Ancient Vedic rituals like Havans form an important part of this process. These ancient fire rituals help invoke the divine presence and generate an atmosphere of sacredness. Group darshans with Sri Bhagavan at the Oneness University campus, varadaiahpalem instill deep love, sacredness and inner stillness in the participants. These darshans are memorable events for every participant, for in the presence of the Divine avatars, Sri Bhagavan and Amma, There is an upsurge of divine grace, love and an immense healing of the heart. Bhajans (devotional songs) in praise of the divine awaken the child within, thus enhancing one's personal communion with his/her personal God. The Oneness Process integrates empirical understanding of teachings with devotion and prayer, thus making it a complete spiritual experience.

∾

Phala Deeksha:

It is a three day course oriented towards discovering causeless love and limitless joy. It helps you achieve success and is designed to clear away hurdles and blocks that might crop up in one's material or spiritual progress.

- The participants get in touch with their destructive unconscious patterns and emotions, get liberated from them.

- They get rid of accumulated hurts and discover a state of forgiveness. When relationships are set right, all other aspects of life fall into place.

- They attain to success and harmony in relationships.

- They are set on the path of self-discovery and God-realisation.

- Special prayers are offered to Sri Bhagavan towards the liberation of one's ancestors.

∾

Youth Deeksha:

A six day course that empowers the youth for a successful future by activating their latent brain potentials which leads to the flowering of their heart and intelligence.

- They overcome fear complexes leading to self-confidence and a positive outlook on life. They discover their early childhood traumas and recreate their destiny.

- Various brain centres are activated thereby enhancing memory, concentration, creativity and intelligence, through the special deekshas for the youth.

- Sets right the relationship with the parents.
- Awakens the emotional intelligence.

- The nagging problems of inferiority, and low self-esteem are dissolved.

- They become successful and happy.

- Inculcates a sense of leadership and responsibility.

- They get in touch with their own higher sacred self or higher intelligence that later begins to guide them.

- They learn the art of being able to access divine grace whenever necessary.

∾

Mahadeeksha:

Where the seekers chosen by the University move ahead on the path of Oneness and God Realisation. This is exclusively for those who are committed to serving man nad God alike.

∾

Contact Information

World Head Quarters ,
The Oneness University,
Varadaiahpalem, Chittor District,
Pin 517 541, Andhra Pradesh, India.
Ph: (08576) 279948 / 58

The Oneness Temple,
Golden City 1,
Bathlavallam Village, Chilamattor Post,
Varadiahpalem Mandal, Chittor Dist.,
Andhra Pradesh, India.
Ph: Ph: (08576) 279966 / 54

Sri Amma Bhagavan Aalayam
Nemam, Andersonpet, (via Tirumazhisai),
Nemam – 602107, Tamil Nadu, India.
Ph: (044) 26273354/26490581

Forth coming releases

A manual instructing to guide people on conducting satsangs.

Contains the phenomenal experiences bestowed by Sri Bhagvan on the seekers

A series that features, for the first time, answers of Sri Bhagavan to frequently asked questions on a plethora of subjects like Love, Relationships, Youth, Oneness etc. Listening to Sri Bhagavan itself would act as Deeksha.